M000198019

# Quit Your Job in 6 Months

## Book 2: Internet Business Blueprint (Formulating Your Business Plan for Quick, Efficient Results)

By: Buck Flogging

www.QuitN6.com

# Companion eCourse

There is a companion eCourse to this book series with over 10 hours of material. Find out more by going to www.QuitN6.com.

# Disclaimer

By reading this book, you are guaranteed to become the most richest motherfucker ever to live ever.

I'm kidding, I'm kidding.

By reading any of my books or enrolling in one my courses, you are obviously not guaranteed to succeed. I do everything in my power to give you the most accurate and foolproof information possible, but that should not be interpreted as a promise or guarantee. No one could ever make a promise or guarantee like that. I have had success myself, and I believe that some of the tactics, strategies, and practices that I used are applicable to many others looking to launch and operate a successful business, which is why I'm sharing that information. But I can't make any promises.

Any business, financial, or vocational decision you make is something that you do at your own risk, and you are ultimately the one responsible for the positive and negative outcomes of those decisions. You should perform your own due diligence and use your own best judgment prior to making any investment decision pertaining to your business. By virtue of reading this book series or interacting with any portion of www.QuitN6.com, you agree that you're fully responsible for the investments you make and any outcomes that may result.

# Table of Contents

# The Proper Order

M ost of you read Book 1 (if you haven't, register at www.QuitN6.com and I'll send it to you for free plus two others), and you were all fired up to start rocking. One idea in your head and you've wet yourself. That's not how to go about it at all.

Treat your online business like a restaurant. Don't send a bunch of customers over before you have a stove, tables, and food to serve. Don't do backflips out in the parking lot and blare peppy music from the loudspeakers, only to have those customers come in and stare at the wall in an empty building.

And, in keeping with the restaurant metaphor, what should you do before you even decide the restaurant name, rent out the building, and buy all the equipment?

You should learn how to fucking cook! And you do that by getting lots of experience, eating at a ton of restaurants to see what they're doing, and doing tons of research on the subject.

Here are the 15 proper big picture steps to developing and launching an internet business effectively, for rapid, reliable results. We'll be discussing the first six in this book:

1. Figure out what you like to do and are good at
2. Brainstorm for ideas that will work
3. Research your ass off
4. Make projections
5. Get all your stuff ready for sale
6. Name and brand your business
7. Create your email subscriber sequence
8. Design site
9. Write content (about page, sales pages, affiliate landing page, books, etc.)
10. Launch business
11. Create affiliate program
12. Start building relationships
13. Drive traffic
14. Get to $100 per day
15. Quit your fucking job

# It Starts with What

> *"I know, I'll read some books and then discuss my findings and my thoughts on a blog."*

That was the extent of my first online business plan. Pretty dumb huh? Yet, I became successful nonetheless. Actually, there were several things that were absolutely right on the money with my "business plan," which of course, wasn't a business plan at all. Rather, it was a plan to spend my free time exploring a topic I found interesting instead of wasting it on mindless entertainment—usually of the Netflix variety.

Author Simon Sinek has a statement that he's made famous, which is, "It starts with why." His speech on this is one of the most famous of the modern era, with well over 1 million views on YouTube. My bad summary of that statement is basically that great things are an extension of some kind of cause or mission. I couldn't disagree more. In fact, the people I know that are most motivated by a cause are usually the ones that, when it comes to launching a successful endeavor, are the least successful. They are really great at daydreaming about how they are going to save the world, but they come up short on taking action.

And that's because a cause of some kind isn't enough. Even going after some kind of cause or mission is usually an extension of wanting to stroke thy ego. Now I know, many of you are thinking that wanting to help others is an act of altruism, and that people who reach out and sacrifice themselves for others are true heroes. Selfless. The opposite of being egocentric.

And that's where I roll my eyes. There are no people free of ego, and nothing strokes the ego more—not money, not sexual attention, not fame—than being thought of as a hero, reaching out and touching other people's lives and making them better. Ending suffering.

We all want to help other people. We want them to like and appreciate us. We want to have an impact. We all have a long list of whys. And we all feel amazing whenever someone praises and thanks us for the awesome, helpful thing we did.

But to really help others in a significant way, we must cultivate the ability to deliver tremendous value. To do that, we must cultivate amazing talent, skills, knowledge, and expertise. This is why the "why" doesn't work. You may want to cure cancer and end the suffering of millions of people. You may daydream about it and totally get off on the thought (ego masturbation). But if you don't like doing research, spending time in a laboratory, applying for grants, and immersing yourself in medical literature—you're not going to be able to fulfill your goals of curing cancer. It doesn't matter how bad you want to do that, if you don't get off on the how and what, the why isn't enough to trump that.

Instead, start with what. Coming up shortly are some "what" questions. I want you to actually answer every single one of these questions. I want you to put the book down and ponder them for hours or even days and weeks if necessary. The answer to these questions will help guide you to the most important aspect of planning your business, which is finding out what you like to do and who you are.

*Not who you want to be or who you ought to be, but who you are.*

Because the greatest key to success in any business is follow-through, and the great secret to follow-through is enjoyment. If you enjoy what you're doing, you'll do it more, do it harder, be happier while you're doing it, and develop a shitload of value in the process. At the end of it all, you'll have such great skills and expertise that you can't help but make other people's lives better. You will serve them. But to serve others, you have to be awesome at what you do, and to be awesome at something, you have to do it relentlessly with gusto and glee for years and even decades to reach true greatness.

That won't happen if you're focused on helping others. You need to be focused on your own shit, for no other reason than "because it's fun" or "because it's so intriguing I can't *not* do it."

Without further ado, here are the big "what" questions for you (and a couple hows and whens):

- What are you good at?
- What do you like doing?
- What is your favorite hobby?
- What would you do with your life if you had $50,000 deposited into your bank account every month and money was not an issue?
- What books are you unable to put down when you're reading them?
- In what area do you have exceptional memory/recall?
- When you have extra money, what do you spend it on?
- When you go to a shopping mall, what stores do you typically wander into?
- What will keep you up at night if you think about it right before you go to bed?
- What kind of books do you read?
- When you have conversations with others, what do you steer the conversations toward?
- What do you always make time for?
- What do you like to do that others might consider work?
- How do you spend your free time?
- What gifts do you ask for on holidays?

Answer these questions carefully my friends. For some of you, the first few questions will be enough to extract an obvious answer to the question of what your business should be about. For others, it might be a lot more difficult. Not everyone has clear obsessions with certain, specific things. Also, many of you will have obsessions that are current but haven't lasted that long, or a pattern of being really interested in something for a while and then moving on. That's me for sure. My interests are always meandering and weaving in new directions all the time, but there are some things that never go away, such as enjoying writing or spending time in the outdoors.

When I went through some of these questions, it took a little while to figure things out. I didn't have clarity for months really. But when I knew, I knew. I felt that hunger for knowledge, and when I dove in and pursued those curiosities, my curiosities grew into an obsession. I followed that obsession, and in that time I became, like I mentioned in the first book, a very knowledgeable scholar that ended up helping many hundreds of thousands of people to improve their health—in small and large ways depending on who they were.

I enjoyed every second of it. And ONLY because I enjoyed it so much did I create enough value to serve others and make money. I know it's not about the why, because I never had any strong desire to help anyone with anything. My pursuit of knowledge in health and nutrition specifically was more like a gamer playing Minecraft or someone trying to figure out how to solve a Rubik's Cube. There was no "why" at all. I just did "what" I wanted to do, and tried to spend as little time as possible doing what I didn't want to do.

What an easy path that is to take! Whether you make money or help others or not doesn't really matter. You can't lose, because nothing matters more in life than spending as much of your time as possible doing what you love to do. That's the biggest determinant of the quality of your life, without question.

Actually, we should all have exactly the same "why." *Because that's what we love to fucking do.*

And that's good enough. You may want to solve world hunger or save the whales. But if you love to write and perform music, and you do it well, then you're just going to have to contribute to society by entertaining them with wonderful music, enjoy your life in the process, and let someone else worry about whales and hungry people.

In reality, because we all tend to go much farther much faster, and become much wealthier, by relentlessly doing what we love—your greatest contribution to feeding the hungry and saving the whales will probably be by becoming a great musician and donating a ton of money to your causes.

Be authentically you. Without regret. Without remorse. If you get on the same page with your true desires and feed those desires a steady diet of what they want, you'll live a rich, fulfilling, successful life—you'll serve others, and you'll make the maximum contribution to whatever causes you're most inspired by.

Once you're fairly clear about what excites you, and how that ties into what you're best at or most knowledgeable about, move on to the next chapter and start mapping out a strategy for how you can make a living following that path.

# Business Brainstorm

I get it. You're passionate about baseball. But your fastball is 62 MPH, and it takes you two full minutes to touch all four bases. Doesn't look like you'll be turning pro no matter how many hours you spend out in the back yard throwing balls through the tire hanging from the tree.

What we like doing isn't always what we're good at. But there's usually some way to integrate the skills we do have in an area that we love, or vice versa—integrate something we love into our skills.

I'll let you figure that out for yourself with a little brainstorming. But don't give up until it feels right. Don't give up until you come up with an idea that keeps you up all night and makes you really hate work the following day, and not just because you're tired.

When you start to have some idea about what you want to do, and what you can do, it's time to finally start thinking about how to translate that into a reliable income that covers your basic living expenses with a little left over.

I'm a fan of figuring out ways to at least get to the "Golden Point" of $100 per day (once you get there, you know you're golden) as quickly as possible, in fewer than six months ideally. That's a pivotal point, because at that point you can feel confident in quitting the day job and immersing yourself fully into your new, entrepreneurial endeavor. When you do that, your success will really take off. If you can reach $100 per day while maintaining a full-time job, imagine what would happen if you freed up those 40 hours and were able to dedicate most of them to your own business.

So in the strategizing tips we discuss, I'll be focusing on things that will get the quickest and most noticeable results with the fewest hours. My focus will not be on long-term strategies and actions that will pay off years down the road, but that won't deliver much revenue at all in the short-term, such as blogging (although this can still work for some, depending on your business model). I may have made a big statement against blogging in naming myself Buck Flogging, but I'm smart enough to know when it still can be a strong asset, or even the backbone, of a successful online business.

I hate having to write about planning an online business, because I have to speak in generalities. That kills me, as each business will likely need a great deal of customization to get all the pieces to fit, and I just can't go into all of that. It's not feasible. But let's see what we can do.

Let's say you're a decent writer, and you enjoy writing. If so, you're lucky. Success online is a walk in the park for good, prolific writers. Right there you should feel 100% confident that you'll be successful if you set things up intelligently so that you can stand out amongst the thousands of other bloggers and authors out there.

So you'll be doing some writing. And let's say that you are just wild about gardening. You love working in the soil, and you're an experienced home gardener. You even worked at a nursery over the summer in college because you loved being outside and working with plants. You can't imagine a better reality than to quit going into the insurance office that you work at 40 hours a week and turn your attention towards an all-out gardening geekfest.

The typical setup for most blogs in this space, and others, is to write articles and maybe write a book or two about gardening. Then go nuts over on social media trying to get readers over to your site to check your stuff out.

You can be successful doing exactly that. Maybe even very successful if you really are the bomb in the garden and can write with some serious personality and flavor to keep things really fun for readers. But it's probably going to take forever, and if you aren't exceptional as a gardener and/or a writer, the odds are not in your favor. Get ready to permanently join the under $500 per month club, which Darren Rowse, Lord of blogging, estimates to be 70% of all bloggers.

Hmmm. This doesn't look like a very good strategy. Plus, gardening, while popular, just isn't popular enough to make a good living off of a few ads and a couple of books. The most popular site looks to be Mother Nature Network, and they've expanded way beyond gardening, probably for good reason.

What to do?

Clearly writing some blog posts to an audience of what will likely be less than 1,000 people for a couple years, with nothing to monetize the site other than ads and an eBook or two of yours, isn't going to pay the bills. And if you're not making any money, you won't have enough fuel to start making some *real* money.

Please, for the love of all that's holy, don't just fire up a blog on Wordpress and start hacking away! I don't care what a friend of this woman you know did with her blog! You can do better. I don't care if your blogger friend of a friend has made millions, you can probably make more money in less time on less traffic, provide more real value, and have more fun.

To be sure, blogging is just one way to drive in some traffic—one of ten primary ways that we'll discuss in Book 3. The name Buck Flogging should hint at where blogging falls on that list.

With a few affiliate links here and there and some ads displayed on the site, you might make a few pennies per visitor. If you've got a couple of books for sale and people like your writing, you might be able to get as much as 5-10 cents per site visitor, but it's still not enough. Here's a better plan, and one that's much better suited to quick success.

Start with a book. Write the most epic book you know how to write. Give away as much quality information as you can. Be really cool in the book. Let your personality shine through. Make it super fun and engaging to read so that some people will form a strong connection to you. You don't have to please everyone, you just have to be really awesome in some people's eyes. That's better than being bland and just delivering some information, staying in the background. Edit the crap out of it. Really make it a quality work. This will be your lead capture bait, as we'll discuss in Book 3.

Now that you've got a great introduction for people—a piece of work that wows them and allows them to get to know and connect with you with their very first exposure to you—you now need to create a few things for sale at various price points. One for under $50, something for $100-500, and something around $1,000 or even higher—or some similar combination.

Actually, for gardening specifically, which is something that is heavily-dependent on supplies and physical products, I'd think you'd want to have a combination of digital and physical products on offer. Maybe even a whole storefront of seeds, soil minerals, tools, and supplies.

If that sounds like too much trouble, you could at least identify about 20-30 things for sale that you really love. Maybe that's bat guano as a fertilizer, some special kind of gardening gloves, the tubing for drip irrigation, a certain brand of seeds or particular heirloom varieties, and so on. Or maybe you create an amazing collection of 20 different things that help new gardeners get off to a blazing start, with rapid improvements in their soil quality. Find out where all of these things are sold online, which ones have an affiliate program, and start signing up. Or at least pick your favorite company and promote their products as an affiliate over others.

But you should try to create your own product of some kind as well, such as a digital how-to video course on composting or building raised beds with an upsell to do consultations for helping gardeners troubleshoot what's wrong with their soil and garden. You know there are tons of beginner gardeners out there that think they're doing everything right but keep having all their leaves turn yellow, or having insects attack everything. They need someone with experience to help guide them, and that can be you.

You might even throw out the possibility of travelling to help people get started or troubleshoot their gardening issues. Or you could host a workshop in your area. There are so many things you can do. This is just what five minutes of me brainstorming about it can come up with. I'm sure you can do better.

But the important point to make here is that you need a way to:

1. Build rapport and trust with people that find you
2. Sell them something inexpensive that wows them
3. Sell them something more expensive that wows them
4. Sell them something even more expensive that wows them

You may think it's ridiculous to charge over $1,000 for something, but if you get people liking you, trusting you, and noticing tangible benefits from putting your advice into practice, you better have the full works available for them to purchase, or else you might be missing out on a lot of extra money.

I get it. I'm focusing too much on money. You'd be fine just making some money off of your eBooks and maybe a little affiliate commission on seeds and supplies. I get that. I was like that, too, for my first six years online. But that's a huge mistake that's going to hinder your ability to reach people, be heard, and be helpful. Don't do that. Money is your greatest asset for reaching people. Here's why:

All of that money you make on the back end after giving away that free book allows you to make a lot of money per visitor. If you make a lot of money per visitor, then you can create a great affiliate program. If you do that, then every gardening website on the planet will want to sign up and send traffic your way. A hundred bloggers that have spent years building a following will send over as many members of their hard-earned audience as they possibly can in an instant.

You're in business now!

Not only that, but you will now be serving the entire gardening community. The bloggers will all know, love, and trust you—and be ready to collaborate on all kinds of stuff. You see, all the bloggers out there are looking for a fresh, new, gardening-related thing they can promote and make money from. If you create that, not only will you be serving your following of aspiring and frustrated gardeners, you'll be bringing great value to your colleagues as well. If you thought making friends at work or at yoga class was fun, wait until you start making friends with people that love gardening as much as you do!

And that money! You'll have money to advertise, you'll have money to hire help growing your social media outlets, you'll have money to attend conferences and trade shows and network with even more gardening bloggers and entrepreneurs, and you'll have enough money to get an amazing video camera and launch an awesome YouTube channel. You'll get guest post invites, podcast invites, and the list goes on. And you'll be ready to sit down and write book 2, this time launching it on Amazon and turning it into an instant bestseller because you've got the whole horde of gardening geeks online on your email list. I can see it all now.

If it "starts with what," the next step is money. They say it takes money to make money. I wouldn't say that's absolutely true, but it is definitely easy to inject money into a very profitable business online that makes a lot of money per site visitor, and have it come back to you fatter.

Okay, another very random Buck Flogging example I know. But hopefully you can start to think similarly about an endeavor that you've got kicking around inside your brain—and brain up a storm! Like I said in Book 1, there are several different types of businesses and ways to make money online and off, and a gardening website may be galaxies away from your interests and skillsets, but some themes are universal, and apply to every endeavor.

If I had some universal themes that I wanted to impart on you about designing your own business and being successful in anything that you do, I'd have to emphasize the following the most:

**1.** Be bold and loud. Put yourself out there. Don't be timid. Be true to yourself, but don't shy away from making noise or be afraid to upset someone. You can't whisper your way to success. You really have to stick your neck out there, to the point of feeling slightly uncomfortable at times, to garner quality, engaged attention. When you're brainstorming for business ideas, really identify who you're going to be and how you're going to be. Find other examples of famous people and authorities that have a presentation style and personality that you just find irresistible, and think about how you could be more like that.

**2.** Be radically sincere, and be willing to bend over backwards and do all kinds of stuff—for free even— to make a great impression on both potential customers and potential collaborators. You have to stand out, and you have to earn the trust of others. So you have to always be taking it a step or two beyond what a typical person would do. Just like you, the majority of those people will feel obligated to repay you somehow, either by recommending you and your work to others or by buying your products.

**3.** Design your business in a way that your daily activities are so enjoyable and fulfilling that you'd actually do them for free if no one was willing to pay you. You'll need this to transmit excitement to your customers and clients, you'll need this to make strong connections with the right people, and you'll need this to have the staying power to reach the point of real success. If you don't love it, you're unlikely to keep up with it long enough to be successful, or have the charisma needed to get there either.

**4.** Be extremely greedy when the time is right. You might be willing to do stuff for free because you love it so much, and it might make a lot of sense to give your affiliates a jaw-droppingly generous portion of your sales, but don't forget, once you've worked so hard to position yourself as a trustworthy savant in your field, to wring every fucking nickel out of those relationships that you've built. That will benefit you, your affiliates, allow you to reach and deliver value to more people in the future, and afford you even more unforeseen opportunities as you reinvest that money back into your business.

**5.** Don't jump into anything unprepared! The rest of this book will be dedicated to proper preparedness. It's the most difficult and tedious thing you'll have to go through, but it's worth it.

As I look back at this chapter so far, I'm feeling like something is missing. In fact, after I wrote it, the next morning I woke up and felt sick about it.

---

*How can I help guide them to better brainstorming? I thought. That whole tangent about the gardening website business probably seems a little far-fetched, and with enough moving parts to give them an anxiety attack just thinking about putting all of those pieces together.*

---

So let's take some time to brainstorm together about another couple of examples at least—some very different examples.

First, let's go back to the gardening example I used above. What if that person really just wants to write? They don't want to go through all that to create a successful business, and they don't have anywhere near the expertise they'd need to be doing any kind of consultations or courses. How could they just dive right in to researching and writing about gardening?

One thing you (sorry, switching back to 2nd person, makes it easier for me to think) could do is research all of the gardening blogs and websites on the internet, compiling a list of at least the top 100 if not the top 1,000 most relevant websites, YouTube channels, podcasts, forums, and groups. Once you've identified those, and you've taken a little time to see if you can figure out how each one of those entities is monetizing their following, you could make a list of the top 10 gardening gurus that look like they could benefit from some written content.

For example, you may find someone on YouTube that's doing great, with 50,000 subscribers and 6 million video views, but their website is a dump with hardly any written content on it, and they haven't published any books at all. You may find ten gardening gurus that fit that description.

Instead of building your own website and going down that route, why not reach out to each one of these entities in the gardening space and offer to do some content writing for them, or even ghostwrite a series of books for them with an agreement to share the proceeds from the books?

Or maybe you just pick your favorite site that doesn't have any books published, and offer to promote their site or products in the books you write if they'd be willing to promote the books heavily when they're released. That will probably be more effective than just writing books yourself without having any promotional power behind their release.

Another idea still might be to reach out to people that you think could benefit from some written content to get more traffic, more subscribers, and more customers for their products, and just offer to write some content for them for free on a trial basis. If they start to see some improvement from the numbers and clearly see that what you're doing is helping them, you could take the next step and figure out a way for you to be fairly compensated for your work. I could see you sending out a bulk email to dozens of established gardening powerhouses online that says something like this:

"Hi. I'm Sandy, and I looooovvvve gardening. I know I'm preaching to the choir here, but just had to belt that out.

Gardening is my love and passion, and I love to write (and one of my parents and both of my dogs think I'm really great at it!). I see that you've got a great following on YouTube, but you don't have much of a blog going, or any books or anything.

I figured, like sane people, you probably hate writing and/or aren't very good at it. That's why I thought I'd reach out to you and see if you need some help. I'd be happy to write some free articles for you that you can share on social media. I think it would really help you get more people to your website, get more subscribers, and get more students enrolled in your video course.

If it works, hey, I'll keep it up and we can figure out what it's worth to you to have me as your keyboardtappin' sidekick. And if it doesn't, well, you're not out a nickel.

Give me a call if you want to talk about it. I have a day job (grumbles), so it will have to be after 5pm eastern time on weekdays."

That's a fun email. You'd get some responses, and it probably wouldn't take long before you'd be spending your free time writing about gardening, and not long after that you'd get paid enough for it that you could quit the ol' day job and be part of something much more inspiring.

Or maybe you brand yourself as "The Gardening Ghostwriter" and build a simple one-page website where people can contact you and discuss potential projects and rates, and then reach out to various people in the gardening space that you know need content and strike up some deals—both for content and for books.

I'm certain you could be writing $100 worth of content every day for one or several gardening internet businesses in a reasonable amount of time.

Okay, let's move on from gardening. I'm much more likely to get into a gardener than I am a garden anyway. I may not get any dirt on my hands, but I can still get dirty! Buck Flogging. Plowing fields since 1992!

Alright I'll stop.

Now let's say your skills are nonexistent. Yes, you speak English and can count without using your fingers, but that's about the extent of it. Let's brainstorm about something valuable that you could learn and like doing in a reasonable amount of time online:

You could learn to make Slideshares. You'll learn more about Slideshare later, because it's a pretty cool place (although weird as hell), for people starting out online to reach a lot of people quickly. Basically you create about a dozen sentences to describe something, and overlay each one on an image. At the end, you put a link to a lead capture page. You can see one Mrs. Flogging made for me here: http://bit.ly/1geWPAT. Slideshare is a totally viable way to get email subscribers (I find a slideshow posted on Slideshare is good for at least 10 email subscribers), and for some businesses, email subscribers are incredibly valuable. This would be such an easy thing to learn, and it would be a breeze to find clients that would pay you $30 or so per slideshow. Do five per week for about five different businesses and you're golden—later expanding this to a business with a team of Slideshare creators servicing hundreds of businesses.

Another thing you could do is become a quick master of something like PowToon, which is one of several animation tools that can be used to create cute little videos using drag and drop characters and effects. Tons of businesses could take advantage of having a lot of animated videos, taking the content they already have and repurposing it into a new form that is perfect for uploading to YouTube and sharing on social media. And you could probably take a blog post and turn it into a cute, 3-minute cartoon in about an hour and get paid $30-50 for it. Maybe more depending on how big the website is. Once again, after you're up and thriving in no time, you can immediately expand to bring on several more worker bees and start serving hundreds of businesses that are missing out on profits by not having any video presence.

Alright, hopefully those make the possibility of finding your place online, and finding it quickly, a much more feasible-sounding prospect. If you can pick something that you want to do and really get after it, you're 80% of the way to success. You'll learn the rest as you go.

I'll leave the rest of the brainstorming up to you, but as you toss around ideas, use this idea checklist, and keep this very important statement in the forefront of your mind…

> *Coming up with a good or even great business idea is easy, but it will only work if the actions needed to make that business a success are something you like to do. Otherwise you'll probably burn out before you reach success.*

## Brainstorming Checklist:

- Identify your primary means of generating revenue
- Identify a two, three, and four-figure price point for your products and services, if applicable (For example, a $20 book, $300 course, and $1,000 private coaching program)
- Try to think of at least ten secondary sources of revenue generation, such as ad revenue or affiliate programs

- Picture your ideal customer and find where they congregate online
- Identify several other businesses that do something similar or serve the same customer that you hope to
- Identify how your customers will benefit from your products and services
- Identify the ideal affiliate for your products or services, if applicable
- Identify other businesses that could benefit from your products and services, or the following you plan to build
- Figure out what steps you'll need to take to get started
- Create a list of everything that could go wrong, and what the outcome of things going wrong would be, financially and otherwise
- Come up with a list of business and website names, and write down how each name will help customers connect with you

# Ready, Set, Research

Man, you're gonna hate this chapter, which is saying a lot after the pain and suffering you went through in the last one. I'm a stickler about doing a lot of research before you even think about what your business is going to be called, much less launch the thing. You really have to know what's out there, and there's no better time to find that out than *before* you launch your business.

Once your business is up and running, you won't have a whole lot of time or desire to do research, and in the research process you'll find things that shape your business, and find lots of people that will ultimately build your business for you.

I know you want to dive right in to the exciting part, but you really have to slow your roll and learn absolutely everything about the territory you're moving into first. If you really research to exhaustion, putting in at least a good 100 hours before you even fully decide what your business is and how it's gonna work, your likelihood of being successful, and being successful quickly, is many multiples higher.

I hope you like spreadsheets. If you don't, tough shit. Do your research first whether you like it or not. Then enjoy a lifetime of easy, efficient success and powerful relationships with the right people thereafter. I know I'm all about doing what you love and screwing the rest, but I also had to stop three years in and figure out how to make money, and the research I should have done in the beginning was what I had to do to find a way. Please don't fail for three years because you didn't take the time to prepare. I know, I hate planning, preparing, and research, too. But the result is knowledge, empowerment, and clarity. So do it!

Okay, spread them sheets and let's get it on!

You'll need at least one spreadsheet, and probably five. Here are the spreadsheets that I would highly recommend making, and making a mile long each:

1. Websites, blogs, YouTubers, and podcasters in your niche (find at least a few hundred)
2. Facebook groups, LinkedIn groups, and other forums in your niche (find at least a few dozen)
3. Potential affiliate products and services in your niche (find at least a few dozen)
4. Top 50 traffic sources on top 5 sites in your niche
5. Top 100 search keywords and phrases for the top 5 sites in your niche

On your spreadsheets, keep the information minimal. Don't feel like you need to write down every site's ranking on Alexa, number of Facebook fans, etc. Just leave a link to each place, the name or names of the people that run the joint, and any notes to help you remember them at a glance.

This is a very tedious exercise you bet, but it forces you to do one of the most important things you'll ever do for your business, which is to get to know everyone in your niche. Of course, not all of the sites that you go through will stand out and be memorable, but spend at least five minutes on each one of them just browsing around and looking for things that stand out, taking a moment to see what they're doing to monetize, and assess what you think is working for them and what they might be able to do better.

This process will get you knowing the niche better than almost every one of the people running the businesses you are researching. In some cases, you'll end up knowing a person's business better than they do, by studying the search terms that are working for them and identifying their top traffic sources— something many of them won't even know.

At the end of it all, you'll have a 360-degree bird's eye view of *everything* that is going on in your niche. You'll see what you do and don't like, see some repeating themes and take note, and your brainstorming will be greatly enhanced. Perhaps the greatest asset you'll develop is that you'll see what's missing, how you can be unique, and how you can fill a need in the marketplace.

You'll also be well-armed to do what I consider to be the greatest not-so-secret weapon of mine for quick success—network with the medium-sized influencers in your niche.

There are going to be some big sites, YouTubers, and podcasters in your niche that will be pretty untouchable to an internet business newb like yourself. But for every massively successful person, there will be 10-20 people with a medium-sized audience. They will have attracted a decent-sized loyal following of a few hundred to a few thousand people, but at the same time they won't be so busy and hounded by people trying to get their attention that they won't respond to your emails. They probably will indeed respond to you if you shoot them an email or tweet at them. And you can start building a relationship with them right away, starting first by reaching out and offering to do something to help them out.

Doing this can lead to them becoming an affiliate for you (or you for them or both, or what's called, in internet-marketing-ese: A "JV partnership"), inviting you to guest post on their blog or be a guest on their podcast, or something unpredictable but highly beneficial to you. Striking up some friendly relationships with the right people—the people with an audience of your ideal readers / customers / clients—is the ultimate way to go from zero to the golden point at hyperspeed.

I first experienced this about a year and a half into my blogging adventures. There I was, busily blogging away in secrecy with 50-100 visitors finding me on Google every day, and then, suddenly, a moderator of a decent-size Yahoo group found me. He thought what I was writing about was interesting, so he brought my blog to his group's attention. Immediately

I began getting 300+ visitors to my site every day, and my blog comments went from just a handful or even a total goose egg to as many as 100 comments on every post.

I can't imagine there were more than 500 people in this bizarre and obscure group, but them finding me was a monumental event in my history as an internet entrepreneur. It didn't take but a few more events like this to take me to a point of reasonable success. Knowing what I know now though, I wouldn't have sat waiting for someone like that to find me a couple times per year. Instead, I'd reach out to them immediately. Dozens of them. And boom. With an intelligently-designed business I would have been in good shape within just a couple months of coming out of the gate.

One of the businesses I helped to start recently, Archangel Ink, reached the golden point with three emails to the right people. That's all it took. I found the people at the top of the food chain, reached out to them, did them a favor, showed them the value in our services, and the next thing I knew they were telling people about us. We were hit so hard with business that the most difficult thing we faced was expanding from three of us to more than ten in a period of just a few weeks.

Three emails did that!

With a better staff in place ready to handle a massive volume of work, I would have sent out a hundred emails like that, hitting up absolutely every person with any size following of our ideal customers. Instead, I just hit up a few of the big ones (but not the biggest ones, because, like I said, you really can't expect to engage a big-timer when you're just starting out—but you'll get them later after you've built a solid reputation).

Take a special note of this. Go to the top of the food chain when you're starting out. Don't try to connect with your audience/customers, try to connect with the people that have spent years accumulating an audience of your customers. It's much more efficient. Like a vacuum cleaner, you can suck up their audiences one by one and quickly become a powerhouse in your space. And, if you have a smart business that brings in $10 or more per email subscriber that you get, you can create an attractive affiliate program and accelerate the rate at which everyone in your niche is driving traffic and customers over to you.

And I don't mean to make it sound like you are trying to con people into stealing their audiences away. It's the internet. The internet just doesn't work like that. I want you to be genuine friends with each and every one of these people. I want you to reach out and help them with sincerity. I want you to think about them and wonder how they're doing. I want you, once you're making more money than they are, to reach out and help them be more successful just as they helped you. Sell their stuff to your audience as an affiliate for them. Spread the love all around.

Sincerity. Authenticity. Integrity. They will take you far. They will take you much farther than being selfish.

Okay, so how are you going to do all this research? I think the only tool you'll really need is Alexa. Alexa is an Amazon company that gathers all kinds of crazy information and data on every website on earth. They have a 7-day trial period on their more advanced data, so if you research about 12 hours a day for that whole week, you might be able to gather everything you need before being charged. Otherwise you'll get hit for $50, but that will give you a whole month, and that should be plenty to gather all the information you need before getting hit for $50 again.

When you're ready to do all your researching on keywords and traffic sources (spreadsheets 4 and 5), start your trial of their "Insight" package at www.alexa.com/plans. That will give you everything you need. But note, you won't need to purchase anything from Alexa to complete spreadsheets 1, 2, and 3, which you should do first before the final two.

Happy researching everyone. I know it's a bitch, but it should also feel pretty damn exciting, it should be very encouraging to your confidence seeing all the others out there doing what you want to do, and the knowledge you gather specific to your niche is power indeed. I'd give anything to go back in time and force myself to do this when I first started out. That's why I'm forcing you to do it. Seriously. Do it.

# Making Revenue Projections

Okay guys, it's time to finally talk dollars and cents. You've heard me make repeated reference to creating a "complete business." You've heard me state something about making sure to set things up in a way where you can get a strong conversion rate on email subscriptions, and then make $10 (or more) off of each of those subscribers on average. You've heard me talk about the "Axis of Income." At least if you read Book 1 like a good little boy or girl you did.

Now it's time to come up with a good plan, assuming you have a more traditional website setup and aren't going out to put on a one-person freelancer show. Nothing wrong with that of course. It's a great starting point for many, and you can use the reputation you build to create a fantastic business later, as we have discussed at length with many random examples.

The first thing you want to do is identify your primary revenue sources—and yes, you still shouldn't have made the final call on the name of your business, your website address, your logo, or any of those particulars yet. That all comes wayyyyy later. You have to make sure you've got a winning idea first, and that all the pieces of the puzzle can be put together. You have to know every site out there and what everyone's up to. Then you can think all you like about how you're going to name it and brand it. Hey, I know you just want to rush out and buy a website and start building it, but going out and buying a website and *then* thinking about what you're going to do with it is absolutely, positively, fucked. So please, don't do it.

By "primary revenue sources," I mean the stuff of yours that you plan to sell. It could be physical products, membership-based subscriptions, eCourses, one-on-one coaching, eBooks, audio seminars, services, or, preferably, a combination of several of them.

Try to split things up as much as you can as well. For example, if you want to put together some kind of course, you should probably break it up into several, such as beginner, intermediate, and advanced. If you want to write a book, if there's a way to split that book up into several volumes, do that. If you have some kind of subscription-based something or other, create multiple levels of membership.

Another thing you'll probably want to do is create the right sequence, that you have control over. Start with something free, then go to your most inexpensive next step, and continue to take your leads through that pipeline until you reach your most expensive item or service. And yes, it's good to take people on a journey on your terms, revealing things all at the right time instead of just directing them towards your "store" without any discretion. Don't show anyone anything for sale until you know they've received enough to be ready to buy something. No one is going to read a half a blog post and then dive across the room to frantically locate their wallet to buy a $1,000 coaching series with you. We'll talk all about proper sequence in Book 3.

Really brainstorm hard here about every conceivable sell and upsell you could possibly offer related to your area of interest and expertise. And no, you don't have to create it all at once at launch, but at least be able to look into future possibilities for the purposes of making projections, which we'll get to in a sec.

Also be thinking of what you could offer as a freebie to get people to subscribe. Think about what has motivated you to subscribe to something before. I don't know about you, but I don't just throw my email out there easily. I ignore almost everything. Most people give away a free eBook or free report of some kind. That can work, especially if you can show them a paperback to convince them it's a real book and not an 8-page piece of crap, and especially if the book is about to be launched (rather than instant access). This sounds more exciting to people for some reason. Sounds "hot" and "new" I guess.

Whatever you do, try to come up with something at least a little bit unique and novel. You don't want it to be too novel though. You want to make sure that the reason people subscribe is because they're interested in you and what you do. Otherwise it's probably a waste to have them on your mailing list. I mean, you can probably get emails by promising to show naked pics of Scarlet Johansson (I wish I had a camera with me that one night we hung out in Bangkok, but oh well), but that's probably not going to help you sell your dog show prep course.

Your conversion rate on a true lead capture page (a page dedicated purely to obtaining someone's email address and nothing else) should be at least 10%, meaning that 10 of every 100 visitors to the page should subscribe. There's no excuse to ever have it be below that. That would only happen if your free offer—your "optin bait"—was extremely poor, or the quality of the traffic coming over was a mismatch for your content.

And with testing, which you should do relentlessly from day 1 with everything you do until you get things good enough to rock and roll, you should be able to get it to 25-50%. I've heard reports from many people of optin rates even higher than that! I've created a couple of lead capture pages that converted at better than 50%, but it doesn't happen every day! Work on it and you might just get there.

Assuming we can use 25-50% conversion rates on lead capture though, let's start crunching some numbers.

Now, you probably won't hit these numbers to start. That's why you test. I'm using these numbers based on targets that I think you will eventually hit with testing and experience. The rest is left up to your likeability, the strength of your message, your reputation, and many other factors that you have less control over. I was talking to Isabel Foxen Duke today via some email exchanges. You wanna see a bad bitch that gets some real badass conversions? Look at the strength, charisma, and professionalism of her basic intro video (hopefully it's still up when you go to see it, I can't guarantee it will be):

www.stopfightingfood.com

She gets right around a 2.4% conversion rate on a $1,275 coaching series. It's unheard of. She gets that because she is incredibly likeable, builds phenomenal trust, is super open and honest, and people that need her services just do backflips to work with her.

Can you imagine? 2.4% conversions on $1,275? That's over $30 per email subscriber, and that's just one product. It boggles the mind.

So that's the best-case scenario. Let's look at something more reasonable.

Use the following conversion rates (on subscribers, not site visitors) for products that fall at the prices listed below:

- Under $10 = 15%
- $10-50 = 10%
- $50-100 = 6%
- $100-200 = 4%
- $200-500 = 1%
- $500-1,000 = .25%
- $1,000-$5,000 = .05%
- Over $5,000 = .01%

To better help you envision how to use those numbers, let's pretend that you have a product on offer at the bottom rung of every one of those ranges for a total of eight offerings. Let's find out how much money you'd get per email subscriber, a very important figure. THE most important number of all.

- $1 X 15% = $.15
- $10 X 10% = $1.00
- $50 X 6% = $3.00
- $100 X 4% = $4.00
- $200 X 1% = $2.00
- $500 X .25% = $1.25
- $1,000 X .05% = $.50
- $5,000 X .01% = $.50

Add those all up and you're looking at an RPS (revenue per subscriber) of $12.40. That's pretty good. Good enough in fact. Sure, there's room for improvement. But that's a great starting point.

Of course, you probably won't have all those different products and services at all of those different price points, but try to hit at least three major price points, preferably one double-digit price, one triple-digit price, and one quadruple-digit price. If you can.

Okay, now that you have your primary revenue per subscriber, you can calculate your revenue per click based on a subscriber conversion rate of 25-50%.

At a 25% conversion rate, each click to your site is worth $3.10 ($12.40 X 25% = $3.10). If you gave your affiliates half of absolutely everything you offer, then your affiliate program would have an average EPC of approximately $1.55 ($3.10/2 = $1.55).

Not bad. Like I said in Book 1, $1.00 is really the bare minimum EPC to have an attractive affiliate program. So $1.55 would be getting into some pretty exciting territory. But if your conversion rate on email subscriptions was on the high side at 50%, you could double those numbers. Your revenue per click would be \$6.20 and your EPC for affiliates would be \$3.10. You pull that off, and you won't just be able to quit your day job, you'll be operating a company likely to be doing 7-figures in revenue annually.

Of course, if you're a real dynamo like Isabel, and/or you do a ton of testing and create an amazing experience for people once they subscribe, you could have much higher conversion rates on the purchase of your products and services, particularly the very expensive ones.

We'll talk about the ins and outs of implementing that successfully in Book 3. For now, let's just keep making some projections about potential revenue for your business. We need to at least know that your business idea *could* be successful—as in, there's a chance.

It's then that you can be confident enough to start taking the steps to building the thing to find out. This is already a huge step in the right direction compared to most people who get online to see if anybody likes them, and if they do, they figure out something to sell to them. A certain percentage of people that find you are going to like you and build a connection with you no matter who you are or what you say. Use what you sell to actually be the fuel to let people find out about you. It allows you to advertise, it attracts affiliates, and gets you off to a raging start—if you get it even close to right.

Now it's time to start identifying secondary sources of revenue. By secondary revenue, I mean ways you make money from things that you don't sell yourself.

For example, I gave this book away for free to my email subscribers by leaving an Amazon Associates affiliate link in my email broadcast about it. When clicked, it sets a 24-hour cookie, ensuring that I get 8.5% on everything that person buys from Amazon during that timeframe—everything from kitty litter to dildos to laundry detergent. I find I usually make about 5-10 cents per click on one of these links depending on what time of year it is (it's lower in the upcoming image because I have the same person clicking multiple links daily, and that waters down that average).

As you can see from my Amazon Associates account, that can add up to be a lot of money! I'm on pace for over 5 million clicks on links in 2015. This is for the first quarter of 2015, and includes links in hundreds of blog posts, links in Buck Books emails, links posted on Facebook, and more. I sneak them in everywhere.

| Q1 2015 ▾ | |
|---|---|
| Last updated: May 6, 2015 | |

**Earnings Summary**

| Total items shipped | 149090 |
|---|---|
| TOTAL EARNINGS * | $49,415.45 |

View full report

**Orders Summary**

| Ordered items | 149638 |
|---|---|
| Clicks | 1389345 |
| Conversion | 10.77% |

View full report

* Combined report for all tracking IDs.

That's just one revenue source, and one easy way to add some extra kwan to your bottom line. There are so many more potential sources of revenue like this it will spin your head all the way around.

Again, you may think it's not worth the bother, or you don't want to "be all about the money." But you have to be! Not taking advantage of secondary revenue sources is like a restaurant just throwing food away. It's wasteful, it hurts the business, and that hurt is felt somewhere eventually. Either you can't hire someone to help you, you can't pay your hired help what they deserve, your affiliates stop promoting your stuff, you have to overcharge customers to make ends meet, you have to cut corners, or what have you.

With that said, let's figure out some secondary revenue sources. Odds are, you can set things up to where you can make even more money from secondary revenue sources than you do from primary revenue sources. When this happens, you can be even more generous with your affiliate program, thus yielding more eager promotion and higher EPC, it creates room in your budget to spend money on advertising, and it opens up room in your budget to hire content writers.

Okay guys, here's a *very* abbreviated list of common options for adding extra revenue streams to what you may be selling yourself:

**Amazon Associates**

We already discussed this. You can get an Amazon Associates account and link to just about anything on their entire site. If you're writing recipes, leave affiliate links to the items you use. If you sell books yourself, leave an affiliate link. If a colleague of yours has a free book on Amazon, recommend that and use an affiliate link. You can even highlight random text phrases in blog posts. In fact, you should do that, leaving at least one Amazon link in just about every piece of written content you put on the web. No one will think much of it. In fact, it's better than recommending it, telling them to buy it, or otherwise make is sound like a sales pitch. That's what I like about Amazon Associates. You can make a little extra money without forcefully selling anything. Just get them to click. Maybe you only make a nickel per post per day, but with 700 posts out there like I have, that could add up to nearly $13,000 a year.

## Google Adsense

Google Adsense is cool. It's not a big moneymaker, but it does help people make an extra penny-ish per pageview. Adsense matches the ads to your content, so the ads should be pretty relevant to what people are reading about. When someone on your site clicks the ad, you get a little chunk of change. If you are planning on having a busy site with blog posts and all, and driving lots of low-grade traffic over there by the thousands, Adsense is something to get up and running as soon as you can.

## Banner ads

Find something that's pretty relevant to the readership you're attracting, such as an affiliate program of some kind, and put a banner ad on your site for it. You can rotate and test different ones, and you may get someone willing to pay per 1000 impressions with more of a straight advertising type of arrangement. I wouldn't overdo these and make your site look like Times Square or anything, but a few can add a little extra revenue to your bottom line.

## Blog sponsorship

If you're writing about something very specific, you may try reaching out to potential advertisers that you think are a perfect match to the audience you draw. In some cases, they may sponsor your entire blog. You'll get a nice monthly check, and you won't have to busy yourself swapping ads in and out and all of that. I've never done this, but for the right business model with very specific content, this could be an excellent way to monetize your site.

## Podcast sponsorship

I mentioned podcast sponsorship already in Book 1. It seems like the going rate is about 2 cents per download. If you have some success and start seeing 100,000+ downloads per month, you can start really making some decent income from podcast sponsorship. But even if you get just a fraction of those downloads, it's still a good idea to get one or more sponsors to help bring in a little extra cheese. It all adds up.

## YouTube video views

For every million views on YouTube you'll get at least a couple thousand bucks, and maybe more if you select more aggressive advertising—putting multiple commercials into each of your videos. I don't think I'd recommend that per se, as ads are super annoying and will probably hurt your brand and engagement for an unjustifiably small chunk of ad revenue, but getting a little bit from your YouTube videos helps. You should set that up, however small your following may be. It all affects your bottom line.

## Udemy

Udemy is a place online that offers tons of classes and courses. I'm envious of their business model. Very genius. Courses in general are thought of as having a very high value, and people will often pay hundreds of dollars to attend courses. Being a hub for courses, therefore, is good business—they take a cut from every class and course purchased by any student. They also have an affiliate program that pays very well. Depending on what your website is all about, there may be a course available—or several perhaps—and sending people over to Udemy to check them out could be a great way to earn extra income. You could even send them over for a free course, and you'll get a commission on other courses they may sign up for. We're just testing out their affiliate program now to find out how viable it is, and we're seeing earnings per click at over 40 cents, which is very high for something that has thousands of things to promote.

## Clickbank

Clickbank is a huge hub of affiliate products, most of them digital in the form of eBooks and courses. You can find an affiliate product or ten to fit just about every niche. Most of them pay 75% to the affiliate, and cost quite a bit. That's great for you. I'd recommend getting a Clickbank account started and getting familiar with what's there. Even promoting just a couple of things per year could add another few percentage points to your bottom line. I made more than $10,000 my first two weeks after opening my Clickbank account. Just don't overdo it, as promoting too many of anything, particularly Clickbank products which often have pretty high-pressure sales videos and squeeze pages, can really burn the trust you've built with your audience.

## Audible

Audible has been one of the most attractive and widespread affiliate programs on the web over the last few years. Users, when they sign up for a free account after clicking on your link, get a couple of free audiobooks, and in doing so they earn you a commission. If they go on to become regular Audible Listener Members, your commission goes up even higher. I was an Audible affiliate for quite a while, but recently they changed things up, and now you can promote the free Audible trial membership directly through Amazon Associates. So check that out once you've got your Amazon Associates account up and running.

## Events

In any niche, there are always events going on throughout the year. This usually takes the form of conferences, summits, online summits (with lots of recorded interviews), book bundles, and more. Most charge a fee to acquire all of the materials and pay 50-75% to the affiliate for promoting the events—more if you are a participant or contributor to one of these events. While these events are becoming a dime a dozen, and the effectiveness of them has been watered down tremendously, they still have some viability. Especially the good ones. Be selective, and promote a couple of the best ones that come along each year in your niche if it's a good fit for your overall business model.

That's a very short sampling of secondary revenue sources that you might be able to capitalize on with your business. The great thing about affiliate programs of all kinds is that they can allow you to sell a ton of products other than just the ones you create yourself, and often you get an even bigger share of the commission than the person hosting the event, course, product, etc. You don't have any of the product development headaches, web design costs, organization headaches, and so forth. You just copy and paste your link into an email broadcast and voila!

Amidst all the excitement though, I must warn you about being overly promotional. Quality trumps quantity on the internet every time, and although I feel like I did indeed shortchange myself on my original business by not promoting any affiliate products unless I had contributed to the offering somehow, I did keep my integrity intact, and that gave me tremendous loyalty and staying power in my niche. Do what feels right. Just remember to be totally authentic. Keep that trust above all else, even if it means sacrificing some short-term revenue. Or else you'll find that the audience you built, no matter how big, will simply stop buying anything that you promote or recommend.

I must share this with you though, which is an email I saved from a very successful internet marketer friend and colleague of mine from years ago. It was an eye-opener for sure. It didn't sink in much at the time, but now I get it, and I should probably print this out (if I remember how, lol) and post it on my wall as some kind of Parable. The Parable of Scooping Up Revenue When It's Right in Front of You.

This guy had hardly any products of his own for sale, used a tactic for capturing email subscribers that we'll talk about in Book 3, and in turn built a 7-figure business sending out a weekly email to his list with various affiliate offers. This is what he wrote as a critique to my "rule" of refusing to promote outside affiliate products. I've anonymized it to keep it from being too revealing:

> *"Dude!*
> *You're leaving MAD money on the table with that rule. I promote other people's shit all the time. Did $75K last week on [affiliate offer]. Did $40K on [another affiliate offer] a few months back. Evidently, my list loves that shit.*
> *You gotta stick to your guns, though. I hear you.*
> *Rules are rules. All good, homie.*
> *But seriously, at some point you may want to rethink it. Reciprocity is HUGE in our line of work. Not that you have to promote bad products, as I only promote good shit. But when you help peeps out, they eventually move a TON of product for you when you have your next launch -- even if your product has nothing to do with them.*
> *Hope that didn't sound lecture-ish. I just hate to see people leave money on the table. The more cash we have, the more impact we can make."*

Let that sink in deep. You must get past this "Oh, I'll just write some blog posts like so and so and make money on the sales of my eBook. If it only winds up being a little bit, that's no big deal. I like my job okay anyway. And that affiliate this and funnel that and EPC stuff just gives me a headache."

If it sounds scary, daunting, and complicated—and you feel a little fear or hesitation about it—then that's EXACTLY what you fucking need to be working on. That's a sign of your weak spot, and you need to fix your weak spot to be the best you can be. And trust me, you'll need to be your best to compete with all the great stuff out there on the internet. You can't halfass it.

Okay, I'm calming down. Breathing deeply now. Counting backwards from ten.

So let's look at how this secondary revenue impacts your Revenue Per Subscriber (RPS).

If you'll recall from earlier, we got a primary revenue source RPS of $12.40 from a rudimentary calculation of multiple products at multiple price points with very modest conversion rates. How will all these secondary sources of revenue impact your total RPS, your ability to make great money, create an attractive affiliate program, and potentially even spend some money on advertising and hired help?

It's impossible to know. Some niches are better than others when it comes to affiliate products and programs. But I think it's safe to say that, armed with a can-do attitude and plenty of research, action, and experimentation, that you'll be able to add at least another 25% to your RPS, and maybe 50% or more. This puts you in the $15.50 to $18.60 range. We'll split the middle and round down to $17.00.

How is that? I think it's phenomenal. It might not be enough to make you a multi-millionaire, but it's enough that you'd almost have to try not to make money to fail. Your affiliate program will be not just more than the $1 EPC minimum, but $2, 3, and even $4 and up. That'll do pig. That'll do.

Yeah, Buck Flogging watched *Babe*. So what? Can't a man watch some talking pigs and sheep?

Most importantly, if you can create all these great revenue streams, thus making a decent amount off of every person you come into intimate contact with on your email list, you can be confident that it's worth sending people to your site.

The Cardinal Sin of many internet businesses is sending a ton of traffic to a site that isn't ready to capitalize on that traffic. I know there are exceptions, like Facebook. Not all sites should be monetized right away. Some are better off just "being cool" and focusing on massive growth. There have been many sites that barely had any monetization going for them at all that were bought out for 10 figures. So what do I know?

But do you really want to be dependent on creating the next Facebook or Instagram to be successful? Do you want to depend on convincing sponsors and investors and such to get you by each month? Or do you want to play it a little safer and go for at least making enough money that you can actually work on your business full-time instead of relegating it to your spare time between work and family? Hopefully you see the advantages, as a small-timer just sticking your toe in the water, of going with the safe numbers— being able to make a living on 100 site visitors per day or fewer instead of depending on being the next big thing.

So that's why I stress the order in which you do things so much, especially in this book.

# Branding, Logo, Domain, and Tagline

The best advice I can give here is to simply wait as long as possible in the business development process to worry about your branding, logo, tagline, domain registration, and all that. It's a kneejerk reaction for me at least to want to jump straight to this part. But every time I do, I end up needing to completely revise my initial idea based on the brainstorming and research phase. Even the tiniest tweak in your game plan can make your original website name a mismatch for the direction you're going to go in armed with this new insight.

Another piece of advice is not to put too terribly much into this either. While name and branding and such is the special sauce for many entities (like Fiverr, for example), most don't live or die by how they've branded themselves, the domain name they chose, and so forth. Logo? As long as it looks professional and has something distinguishing about it that can start to build visual brand recognition for your entity, it will get the job done. Even some of the biggest and most successful companies in history had really mediocre logos. A little "f" on a blue background? Really

Facebook? That's the best you could come up with? That logo wasn't the key to their success I assure you. Neither was the name.

And Pepsi could have just as easily been called Perkle or Jumpsi.

And modern website names are getting weirder and weirder. I swear you could just name your shit Winkysnurf and it would blow up. At the rate people are buying up domain names, that may be the only one left to buy under $10 by 2019, so you better bookmark that one.

If I have anything general that I recommend about your branding and such, it's to try to be really clear and obvious. People just don't look that carefully at things anymore, and we are increasingly left to what we take in with our snap judgments of things. So if you're trying to convey the main point of what you do and connect with someone that might be looking for that, you better try to squeeze it all into your site name and tag line. It better be clear, clever, and punchy. And hopefully memorable, too.

You can see the evolution of my domain selection and branding over the years by the signature line in my emails. They are in reverse chronological order below:

- www.epicwins.us
- www.coursecowboy.com
- www.quitn6.com
- www.buckbooks.net
- www.archangelink.com
- www.180degreehealth.com

Notice how they keep getting shorter and more to the point? Easier to remember? Less nebulous?

I think some of the best stuff I've come up with thus far is the name "Buck Books" and the tagline "Never pay more than a Buck for a book ever again!" It is so absolutely crystal clear what the site is and does. A visitor gets it in two seconds. Nothing confusing or nebulous about it whatsoever.

We're in the testing phase right now, so I may find that my idea is wrong, but I also feel very good about QuitN6. It's quick and clever, and "Quit your job in 6 months" is extremely clear. For those that are interested in pursuing their own venture, it would be appealing. But more so than that is the tag line that we're planning on using, which is "Quit and do your own shit."

**This was the first and only logo mockup my designer made. Good enough.**

It's so very bold, attention-garnering, and in-your-face. Like it or hate it, your ass is going to be captivated by it and remember it. And I'm all about being noticed *and* remembered. That's been a big asset of mine since the beginning, when I put a picture of myself shirtless holding a pig's head in one hand and a large knife in the other across the top of my website. It was an unforgettable image that no one could ignore when they arrived. I was missing a lot of important components, but I've always been masterful at getting people's attention. And I think that's the most important thing. All the tactical knowledge for awesome conversions, search engine optimization, and so forth aren't going to get you nearly as far as the ability to captivate.

How can you be heard? We'll discuss that next.

# Preparing YOU

There are really two things I want to touch on in this final chapter of Book 2: Creating the right online persona and getting psychologically prepared to go make your own luck.

For some reason when I tell Mrs. Flogging that there are two things I want to touch on she rolls her eyes. Can't figure that one out.

As I mentioned in the last chapter, it's good to draw attention and be remembered. This is best done by tapping into people's emotional centers. Tapping into people's emotional centers is about doing something big, bold, unexpected, and at times even radical.

If you're communicating with individuals, such as emailing prospective clients or attempting to make contact with a pivotal influencer in your niche that could help blow the doors off of your business with a few clicks of the mouse, you've got to be different. That's one reason I love reaching out and doing stuff for people for free, and why I like it when people reach out to me in that way as well. It's attention-getting and impressive. It makes you stand out from the rest of the crowd.

I also like being casual and informal enough to actually break the ice and immediately separate myself from all of the other business-ish emails that I know this person gets on a regular basis. My wingman, Willy B. Quitton and I have built some remarkable connections with so many people by being shockingly crude and silly. I mean, are you not like that with your friends and loved ones?

> *If you want to strike up a friendship, communicate like a friend.*

If you want to sound like a stiff business-person and blend in with all the others, then communicate like a business person.

And when it comes to communicating with the masses, I'd strongly recommend turning up the volume on how you express yourself. Sure, there are some successful writers and bloggers and YouTubers and such that write nice, polite, formal stuff. But there are a lot more that write loud, bold, highly-opinionated, funny, quirky, clever, and even mean stuff.

I'm not suggesting that you be inauthentic to how you truly are, but you certainly shouldn't act like you do around strangers. You and I both know that's not the real you at all! The real you bitches and complains and whines and cries over nothing. The real you is emotional and erratic. The real you fantasizes about things you think you shouldn't fantasize about. Foul language escapes your lips when you're really angry. People that don't agree with you are "idiots" (or worse) when no one is listening to you but your husband or wife.

Or is that really just me? It can't be. I know it can't.

We have private personas, and we have public personas.

Funny guy he is. After my own heart for sure.

The point is, you have to be the REAL you. People are drawn to that. It strikes up more debate. It gets spread around. And, like I've been saying all along, it's totally *authentic*. Authenticity is what builds the trust that will be the greatest key to your success—allowing you to make an incredible living for yourself with just a few dozen clients that love you, or a couple thousand readers, viewers, or listeners that adore you.

I always hear morons complaining about how everyone is mean on the internet, and how they would never have the courage to act like that to people in person. That's what's so great about the internet! Finally, we can unapologetically be ourselves, and finally, we can get honest thoughts and opinions from people—all kinds of people, with all kinds of perspectives. It's truly a beautiful thing.

Communicating with people in person feels like a big group meeting of people that have had their reproductive organs removed.

In all seriousness, I think the internet has actually done a great job at showing us who we really are, and allowing us all to develop thicker skins. My debate skills have certainly gotten much better. The secret is simply to welcome, enjoy, and appreciate the internet exactly as it is, and to appreciate and honor who you really are, too.

Be yourself. Take your private persona public. If you do, you'll make a much bigger splash when you waltz out onto the internet hoping to deliver your value to those that can benefit from it.

Lastly, I wanted to also mention getting yourself properly psyched up for pursuing your own endeavor.

You know, I've heard from a lot of people that entrepreneurship just isn't for everyone. Some just can't handle the stress. They'd rather be told what to do. They'd rather someone else take the reins and make all the hard decisions while providing steady income for them to execute repetitive tasks that they already know.

Maybe that's true, maybe it isn't. I don't know.

But I do know that the characteristics of just about any good entrepreneur are characteristics that can be developed. Really, it comes down to just one main characteristic, which is relentlessness.

Relentlessness is steadily moving towards something no matter what obstacles are being thrown your way. Relentlessness is being presented with a difficult challenge and diving right into that challenge, determined to solve the problem no matter what it takes.

An extension from relentlessness is a very optimistic, forward-thinking outlook. The bad stuff doesn't seem that daunting when you almost have a thirst for being challenged by obstacles—knowing how satisfying it is to topple them.

Another extension from relentlessness is that eagerness to take on new things. While challenges may lie on the horizon, fears about those challenges are brushed aside with a "we'll deal with that when we get there" kind of attitude. Those with the quality of relentlessness have a can-do attitude, and tend to attack things with blatant disregard for the consequences.

In other words, relentlessness breeds a general state of mind that sees the positives but disregards the negatives as having much relevance.

There's a downside to this quality, to be sure. Optimism is very dangerous, and can lead to people, even people with thriving businesses, towards reckless decision-making. I know personally that I haven't stopped for a second to think that this QuitN6 program that I'm launching won't be successful. I can't even conceive of how it couldn't be. I know the tactics to make it successful, and my strategy is more informed and refined than all of the successful endeavors I've gotten myself into prior to this one. It's just a matter of simple execution. "Ain't nothin' to it but to do it," Buck says when he's trying to get people to think he's Ronnie Coleman.

If I had $10 million in my bank account, I'd probably blow it all on telling as many people as I can about QuitN6. Reckless yes, but it's hard for me to conceive of failure. And I don't really care that much about money. The success of my projects, beyond the financial aspects, is more important to me than the money itself.

How do you cultivate this quality if you don't have it? I don't know. There's no playbook for it that's for sure. Being aware of it so that you can monitor your own internal dialogue, as well as expose yourself often to someone who shifts your thinking towards much bigger possibilities, is a good place to start. I know that I've been able to talk a ton of people in my life off the ledge of desperation many times, only to right the ship and become much more successful down the road.

I should also point out that I'm just speaking in general terms here. I think we all experience the full spectrum of emotions and thought patterns at one point or another. We all sway back and forth between irrational and unjustified optimism and irrational and unjustified pessimism. I don't mean to make you think that I'm Mr. Nothing Could Ever Go Wrong all the time. I'm not. No one is. Our emotions, by their very nature, are always in motion.

But I guess at the end of the day the ones that pay closer attention to the optimistic visions they have rather than the pessimistic visions they have, are the ones that launch headfirst into their own endeavor. And it's these moronic daredevils that eventually strike gold and end up much wealthier and more fulfilled than those who are more attentive to the fear and doubt they encounter. Because when you get in there and start rolling the dice, you're eventually going to roll a Yahtzee, while those that didn't play at all are left to try their luck in the lottery. And those odds aren't nearly as good as that of an entrepreneur trying things out, testing, learning, fine-tuning, and attacking new opportunity after new opportunity as they arise.

Fuck, I don't know where I was really going with that. All I really wanted to say was this:

**Steps to Entrepreneurial Success:**

1. Irrational optimism
2. Oh shit, this didn't work out nearly as well as I thought it would
3. Cue relentlessness and ability to conquer obstacles and pivot in new directions to find a solution

Don't be rational or you'll never make it past step 1. And you better have resilience and resolve so that you can still believe in yourself and what you're doing enough to fight your way all the way through the difficult Step 2.

I'll leave you with that and see you in Book 3, as we discuss the finer points of email marketing. It may seem simple—hardly worth reading a whole book about. That's where you'd be wrong. Email marketing is an entire galaxy in and of itself. What's inside there will blow your mind, and could likely mean the difference between making a few dollars per email subscriber and forever struggling vs. making $10, $20, or more and becoming a goddamn millionaire.

In conclusion, use what's in this book! Follow it carefully. You only get one chance to launch an internet business, and the information I've covered, while simple, has the power to make all the difference in the world. Do it all, and do it in the right order!

# The Quit Your Job in 6 Months Internet Business Course

Enjoy your Flogging experience? You must have if you made it this far. For a much more in-depth and up-to-date education on launching an internet business with quick and reliable success, take the Quit Your Job in 6 Months Internet Business Course.

Find out more at: www.QuitN6.com